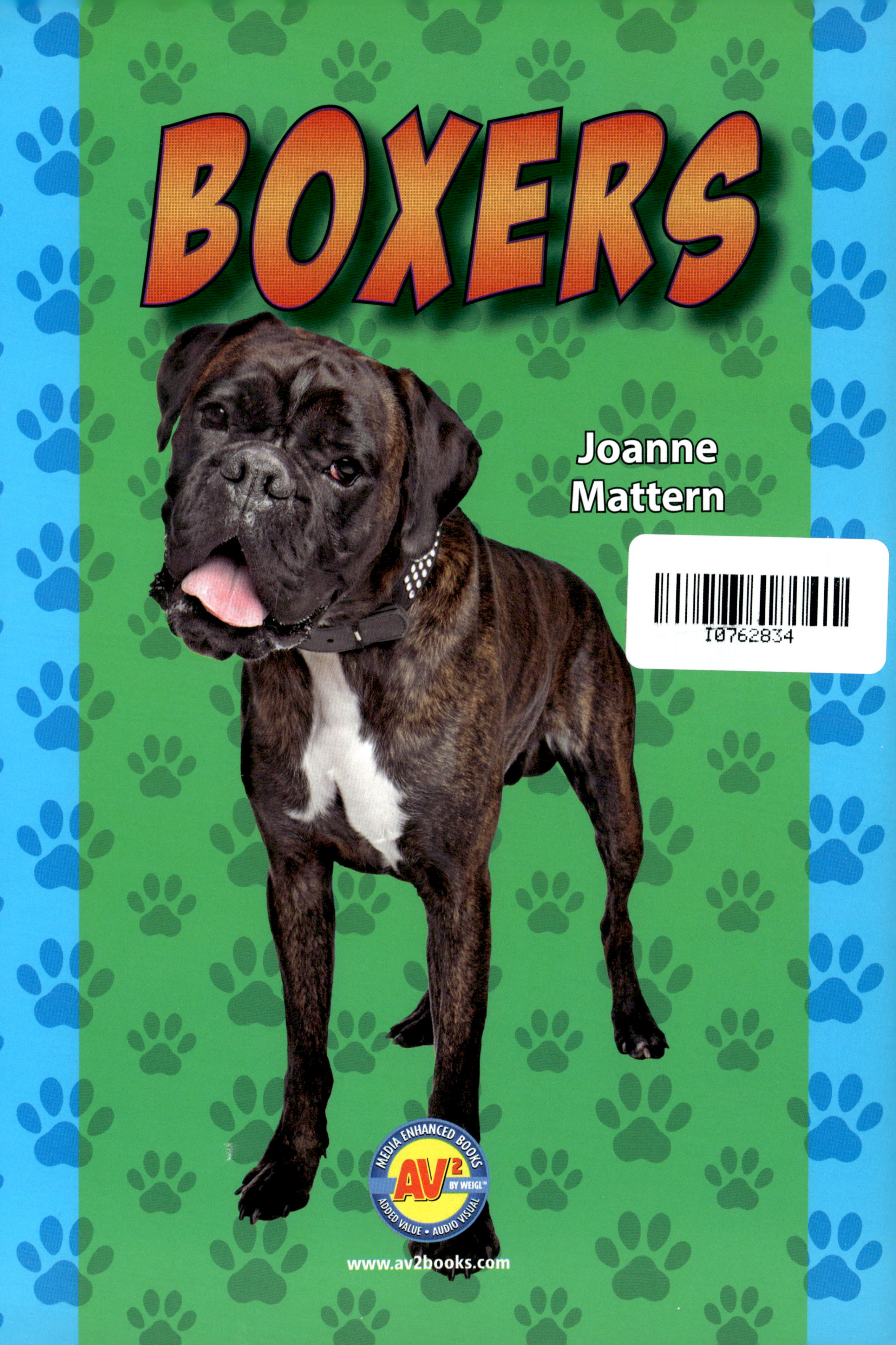
BOXERS
Joanne
Mattern
I0762834
MEDIA ENHANCED BOOKS
AV2
BY WEIGL
ADDED VALUE • AUDIO VISUAL
www.av2books.com

Go to www.av2books.com, and enter this book's unique code.

BOOK CODE

LBK29238

AV² by Weigl brings you media enhanced books that support active learning.

AV² provides enriched content that supplements and complements this book. Weigl's AV² books strive to create inspired learning and engage young minds in a total learning experience.

Your AV² Media Enhanced books come alive with...

Audio
Listen to sections of the book read aloud.

Key Words
Study vocabulary, and complete a matching word activity.

Video
Watch informative video clips.

Quizzes
Test your knowledge.

Embedded Weblinks
Gain additional information for research.

Slide Show
View images and captions, and prepare a presentation.

Try This!
Complete activities and hands-on experiments.

... and much, much more!

Published by AV² by Weigl
350 5th Avenue, 59th Floor
New York, NY 10118
Website: www.av2books.com

Library of Congress Control Number: 2017960030

ISBN 978-1-4896-7366-4 (hardcover)
ISBN 978-1-4896-7959-8 (softcover)
ISBN 978-1-4896-7367-1 (multi-user eBook)

Printed in the United States of America in Brainerd, Minnesota
1 2 3 4 5 6 7 8 9 0 22 21 20 19 18

012018
120817

Project Coordinator: John Willis Art Director: Terry Paulhus

Every reasonable effort has been made to trace ownership and to obtain permission to reprint copyright material. The publisher would be pleased to have any errors or omissions brought to its attention so that they may be corrected in subsequent printings.

Weigl acknowledges Getty Images and Alamy as its primary image suppliers for this title.

BOXERS

Contents

AV² Book Code 2
Name That Dog 4
A Dog That Works Hard.................... 6
Big and Strong 11
A Friend for Life 14
Boxer Puppies 18
Boxers at Work.................................. 23
Caring for a Boxer 27
Boxer Quiz 30
Key Words 31
Index 31
Log on to www.av2books.com...... 32

Name That Dog

What dog is big but likes to cuddle on laps?

What dog served in two World Wars?

What dog likes to jump and dance?

What dog is great at protecting people?

Did you say the boxer?

Then you are correct!

A Dog That Works Hard

Long ago in Germany, a dog called the Bullenbeisser helped people hunt. This large, tough dog chased and caught big animals, such as wild boars, deer, and even bears. Later, Bullenbeissers lived on farms. They herded cattle.

About 150 years ago, a man in Germany started mixing Bullenbeissers with other **breeds**. In time, the dog known as the boxer was created. In 1895, three Germans brought the boxer to a dog show. People loved this new dog.

In 1904, the boxer was recognized by the American Kennel Club (AKC) as an official breed. The AKC creates the **standards** for all dog breeds in the United States. It holds many dog shows to determine which dog is the best. In 1915, a boxer was named champion of an AKC dog show for the first time.

Germany is a country in Europe. It is bordered by many countries, including France, Switzerland, Poland, and the Czech Republic.
Belgium
Germany
Poland
France
Czech Republic
Switzerland
Slovakia
Austria
Hungary
Slovenia
Italy
Croatia
Bosnia and Herzegovina

From 1914 to 1918, many countries fought in World War I. Boxers went to war, too. They traveled with the German army to battlefields all over Europe. They carried messages. They also worked as guard dogs. They helped the soldiers in many ways.

Boxers served in World War II (1939–1945) as well. When U.S. soldiers came home from Germany after the war, they brought some boxers with them. It did not take long before boxers were some of the most popular pets and working dogs in the United States.

The AKC divides dogs into different groups. The boxer is part of the Working Dog Group.

Boxers are known for their large chests and strong muscles.

Big and Strong

Boxers are big dogs. A male boxer is between 22.5 and 25 inches (57 and 63.5 centimeters) tall at the shoulder, and weighs up to 80 pounds (36 kilograms). Females are a little smaller. A female boxer is about 21 to 23.5 inches (53 to 60 cm) tall, and weighs about 60 pounds (27 kg).

Boxers come in different colors. The most common colors are **fawn**, **brindle**, and white. Many boxers have a black mask on their face. Boxers can also have white markings on their face, chest, and legs.

White boxers can get sunburned. It is important to put sunscreen on a boxer's white coat if it is outside.

A boxer has a short, smooth **coat**. Its body is strong. You can see muscles moving under its fur when it runs.

Some boxers have their tails **docked** when they are just a few days old. They have their ears **cropped** when they are about two months old. However, some people think cropping and docking are cruel. Many parts of the world, including Australia, New Zealand, and parts of Europe, have banned cropping and docking. If a boxer's ears are not cropped, they hang down.

Cropped ears and docked tails originally kept dogs safe when they were used for hunting.

A Friend for Life

Boxers are friendly dogs. They love to play. They enjoy chasing tennis balls and flying discs. These big dogs like to run and need a lot of exercise.

Because boxers are smart dogs, they need something to keep them interested. A bored boxer is not a good thing. It can get into mischief. It might chew up shoes or damage property.

Boxers are often called the "Peter Pan" of dogs because they never seem to grow up. Even as adults, they are goofy and playful.

Boxers have been on the AKC's list of the 10 most popular dogs since the early 2000s.

Some people think boxers act like clowns. These dogs love to be silly and have fun. Boxers need plenty of toys. They love to jump. Some boxers even jump up and twist in the air.

Boxers usually like people. These dogs love to be close to their humans. Even though a boxer is a large dog, it will often try to climb onto a person's lap and snuggle. These dogs make wonderful pets for adults. They are also great pets for families with children.

Boxers are very loyal. They will protect their humans. These dogs are alert and always try to keep the people they love safe.

Boxer Puppies

A female boxer can have her first **litter** of puppies when she is between six months and one year old. It takes about 60 days for baby boxers to be ready to be born. Sometimes, the mother will tear up newspapers or towels to make a nest when she is ready to give birth.

There can be between two and 15 boxer puppies in a litter. The average litter size is six to eight puppies. Boxer puppies weigh about 1 pound (0.5 kg) when they are born.

For the first two weeks, boxer puppies cannot be away from their mother. Their eyes and ears are closed, so they cannot see or hear. Boxer mothers feed their babies several times a day. They lick the puppies to clean them.

Boxer puppies double in size in their first three weeks.

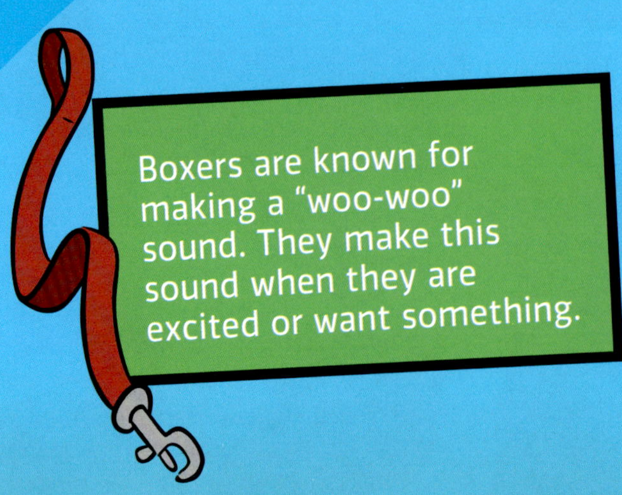

After about two weeks, the puppies' eyes and ears open. Now they can see and hear. They start to make little barks and other sounds. They begin to crawl away from their mother. They are curious about the world around them.

When a boxer puppy is about four weeks old, it can start eating solid food. Puppies like wet food mixed with water. They will still nurse from their mother, too. Later, when their teeth come in, they can start eating dry food.

By the time the puppies are eight weeks old, they are ready to leave their mother. They can begin sleeping in a crate. It is time for the puppies to find new homes.

Growing boxer puppies should be fed about 4 cups (1 liter) of food a day—twice as much food as they will eat as adults.

Skilled boxers can compete in *Schutzhund*, which means "protection dog." This is a competition for tracking, obedience, and protection work.

Boxers at Work

Although boxers love to play, they are also hard workers. Boxers are good therapy dogs. Therapy dogs visit people in hospitals and nursing homes and help make them feel better. Therapy dogs need to be obedient and gentle. Boxers are good at this.

Boxers also make great guard dogs. Guard dogs protect property. They bark if someone tries to break into a business or home. Boxers are not **vicious** dogs, but they are great watchdogs.

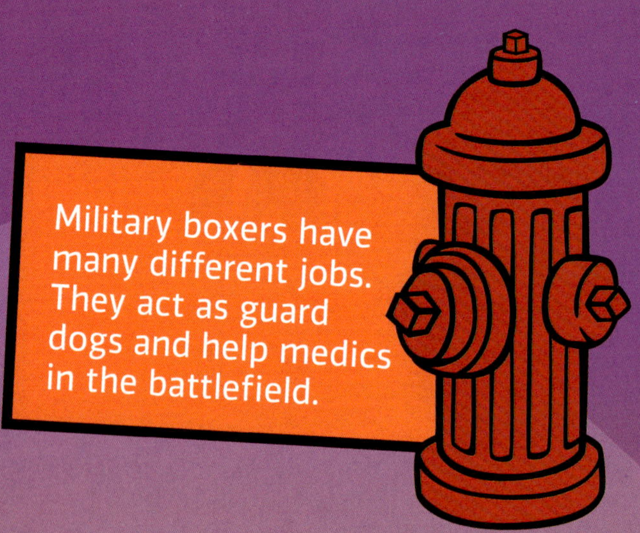

Some boxers work as police dogs. Boxers make good police dogs because of their size and their intelligence. They can learn to perform many useful tasks to help officers in their work. Some dogs are trained to smell certain chemicals. Other police dogs patrol with police officers. They help catch criminals by chasing down and holding suspects. Some boxers wear body armor to protect them during their patrol duties.

Boxers are often used for search-and-rescue work. Their strong sense of smell and hearing allow them to search an area much more quickly than a person.

To stay strong and healthy, a boxer should go for a 30-minute walk at least twice a day.

Caring for a Boxer

Boxers make great pets. However, as with any dog, they need to be taken care of. Before someone gets a boxer, he or she should have everything the dog needs. A boxer needs a collar and leash. An ID tag is also important. A new owner should have food and water dishes, dog food, treats, and toys. A boxer also needs a comfortable bed or crate to sleep in.

All boxers should be trained. Some people take their dogs to obedience classes. Other people train their dogs themselves. Boxers should learn to sit and stay. They should learn to walk nicely on a leash. Some boxers are hard to train. They do not like to do what they are told. However, it is important that boxers **obey** commands so they can stay safe and make good pets.

Owners should keep their boxers clean. Because a boxer has a short coat, it is not hard to take care of. However, a boxer should be brushed at least once a week. It should have a bath every few months. After a bath, a boxer should have its ears cleaned with a wet cotton ball or cloth. This will stop the dog's ears from getting infected. A boxer also needs its nails trimmed every few weeks.

It is very important for boxers to go to the **veterinarian**. They should do this at least once a year. The vet will make sure the boxer is healthy. The vet will also give it shots. These shots protect the boxer from dangerous diseases. Healthy boxers can live to be between 10 and 12 years old.

Boxer puppies should visit the vet once a month until they are about four months old.

Boxer Quiz

Q: When was the boxer recognized as an official breed by the AKC?

A: 1904

Q: What country do boxers come from?

A: Germany

Q: About how many boxer puppies are born in a litter?

A: Six to eight

Q: How long should boxer puppies stay with their mother?

A: About eight weeks

Q: How often should a boxer be brushed?

A: At least once a week

Q: What kind of work can boxers do?

A: Boxers can be police dogs, guard dog, search-and-rescue dogs, and therapy dogs.

Key Words

breeds (BREEDZ): certain types of animal

brindle (BRIN-duhl): brown with black stripes

coat (KOTE): a dog's fur

cropped (KROPT): to have part of the outside of a dog's ear removed

docked (DOCKT): to have part of a dog's tail removed

fawn (FAWN): a shade of brown

litter (LIH-tur): a group of babies born to one animal at the same time

obey (oh-BAY): to do what they are told

standards (STAN-durdz): rules used as a measure to compare animals

veterinarian (vet-uh-rih-NAYR-ee-uhn): a doctor who takes care of animals

vicious (VISH-us): to be cruel or violent on purpose

Index

American Kennel Club (AKC) 6, 9, 16, 30

birth 18

coat 12, 28
colors 11

dog shows 6

ears 12, 13, 18, 20, 28
exercise 14

food 20, 21, 27

Germany 6, 7, 9, 30
guard dogs 5, 9, 23, 24, 30

height 11

life span 28

personality 14, 15, 17
police dogs 24, 30
puppies 18, 19, 20, 21, 29, 30

size 5, 11

therapy dogs 23, 30
training 24, 27

veterinarians 28

weight 11, 18
World War I 9
World War II 9

Log on to www.av2books.com

AV² by Weigl brings you media enhanced books that support active learning. Go to www.av2books.com, and enter the special code found on page 2 of this book. You will gain access to enriched and enhanced content that supplements and complements this book. Content includes video, audio, weblinks, quizzes, a slide show, and activities.

AV² Online Navigation

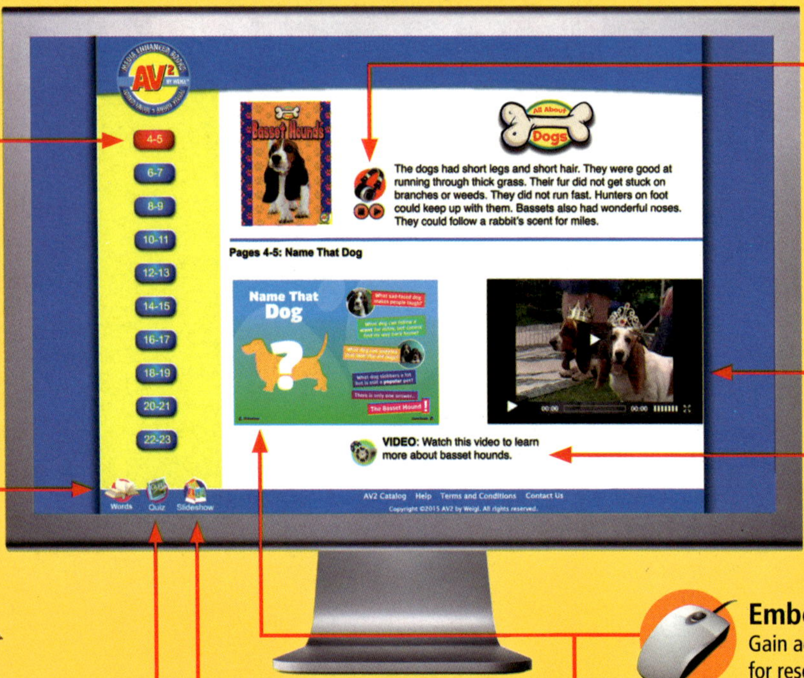

Audio
Listen to sections of the book read aloud.

Book Pages
AV² pages directly correspond to pages in the book.

Video
Watch informative video clips.

Embedded Weblinks
Gain additional information for research.

Key Words
Study vocabulary, and complete a matching word activity.

Try This!
Complete activities and hands-on experiments.

Quizzes
Test your knowledge.

Slide Show
View images and captions, and prepare a presentation.

AV² was built to bridge the gap between print and digital. We encourage you to tell us what you like and what you want to see in the future.

Sign up to be an AV² Ambassador at www.av2books.com/ambassador.

Due to the dynamic nature of the Internet, some of the URLs and activities provided as part of AV² by Weigl may have changed or ceased to exist. AV² by Weigl accepts no responsibility for any such changes. All media enhanced books are regularly monitored to update addresses and sites in a timely manner. Contact AV² by Weigl at 1-866-649-3445 or av2books@weigl.com with any questions, comments, or feedback.